ANIMAL EYES

David M. Schwartz *is an award-winning author of children's books, on a wide variety of topics, loved by children around the world.* Dwight Kuhn's *scientific expertise and artful eye work together with the camera to capture the awesome wonder of the natural world.*

For a free color catalog describing Gareth Stevens Publishing's list of high-quality books and multimedia programs, call 1-800-542-2595 (USA) or 1-800-461-9120 (Canada). Gareth Stevens Publishing's Fax: (414) 225-0377.

Library of Congress Cataloging-in-Publication Data

Schwartz, David M.
    Animal eyes / by David M. Schwartz; photographs by Dwight Kuhn.
        p. cm. — (Look once, look again)
    Includes bibliographical references (p. 23) and index.
    Summary: Introduces, in simple text and photographs, the eyes of crabs, fish, frogs, horseflies, starfish, cats, and geckos.
    ISBN 0-8368-2423-7 (lib. bdg.)
    1. Eye—Juvenile literature. [1. Eye. 2. Animals—Habits and behavior.]
I. Kuhn, Dwight, ill. II. Title. III. Series: Schwartz, David M. Look once, look again.
QL949.S34   1999
573.8'8—dc21   99-18610

SwC
I
573. 88
Schu
13. 10

This North American edition first published in 1999 by
Gareth Stevens Publishing
1555 North RiverCenter Drive, Suite 201
Milwaukee, Wisconsin 53212 USA

First published in the United States in 1998 by Creative Teaching Press, Inc., P.O. Box 6017, Cypress, California, 90630-0017.

Printed in the United States of America

1 2 3 4 5 6 7 8 9 03 02 01 00 99

ANIMAL EYES

by David M. Schwartz
photographs by Dwight Kuhn

A SPRINGBOARDS INTO
SCIENCE
SERIES

Gareth Stevens Publishing
MILWAUKEE

The owner of these eyes
might be looking for
a new shell to call home.

A crab's eyes are perched on little stalks. The stalks can move in any direction. When a crab wants to close its eyes, it pulls the stalks inside its shell. Most crabs grow their own shells, but hermit crabs look for shells left behind by snails.

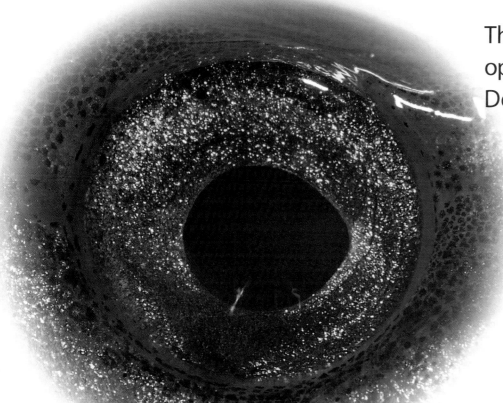

This eye never shuts. It stays open all day and all night. Does that sound "fishy"?

A fish can't close its eyes. It has no eyelids.
A fish also has no tears. Its eyes are washed by water.
With its eyes always open, a fish stays on the lookout for danger.
This male stickleback is pushing its eggs into a nest hole.

Is this a marble
floating in water?

9

No, it's a frog's eye. When a frog blinks, a clear eyelid comes up from the bottom of its eye. To close its eyes, a frog pulls the eyes down into their sockets. A frog can move each eye separately. It can see in two different directions at the same time! This helps the frog stay alert for danger.

These are not fancy sunglasses. They are the eyes of a female fly that bothers horses.

A horsefly looks like it has two giant eyes. Each eye is really hundreds of little eyes. When a horsefly sees a horse, it sees hundreds of horses, but it knows just where to land. Chomp! The female fly gets a meal, and the horse gets a painful bite. Male horseflies feed on nectar and pollen.

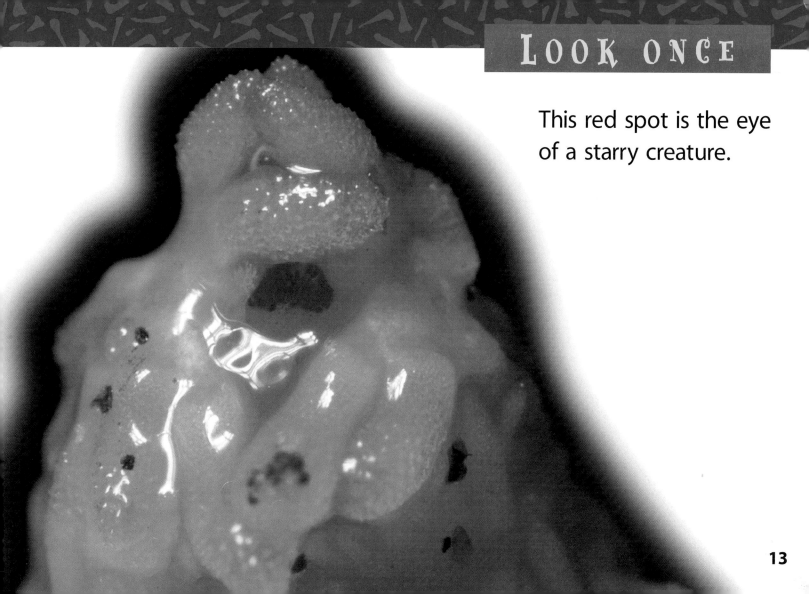

This red spot is the eye of a starry creature.

The starfish, or sea star, has a small, red spot at the tip of each arm. The spots are called eyespots. A starfish uses its eyespots to sense sunlight. Then it moves into the dark shade so predators cannot find it.

These wide, open eyes may be hunting for prey …
or for a warm, friendly lap.

Sometimes a cat's eyes
seem to shine.
Cats have a special shiny
surface inside their eyes.
It helps them see
better in the dark.
At night, cats can see
things people can't see.

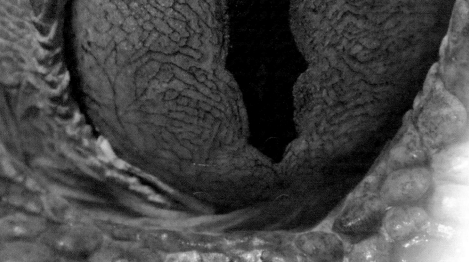

This may look like the eye of a scary beast, but it's the eye of a little lizard people love.

During the day, a gecko's eye is a narrow slit. At night, it opens wide so the gecko can see in the dark. Geckos use their tongues to clean their eyes and keep them moist.

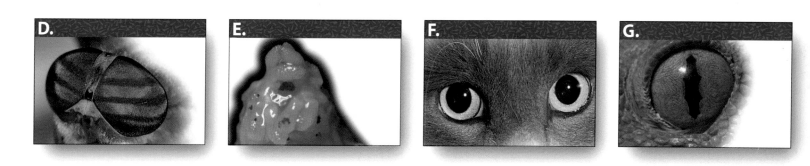

Look closely. Do you know to which animals these eyes belong?

A. Crab

B. Fish

C. Frog

D. Horsefly

E. Starfish

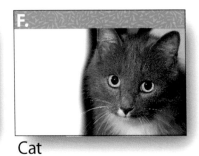

F. Cat

G. Gecko

How many were you able to identify correctly?

alert: quick to notice or act; watching for danger.

eyespot: the small, red spot on the tip of each of a starfish's arms. Eyespots sense sunlight.

gecko: a type of small lizard that eats insects and lives in the tropics.

giant: very large and strong.

lizard: a type of reptile that has a long, scaly body. The gecko is a type of lizard.

moist: wet; damp.

predator: an animal that hunts other animals for food.

prey: an animal that is hunted by other animals for food.

sense (v): to become aware of something through the five senses — hearing, seeing, smelling, tasting, and touching.

separately: apart from others; [done] alone.

shell: the hard, outer covering of some animals, such as crabs and snails, that protects the soft organs inside.

slit: a long, narrow opening.

socket: the hollow part of the face that holds an eye.

starfish: a sea animal that has five or more arms, so that its body looks like a star.

stickleback: a small kind of fish that has several sharp spines.

ACTIVITIES

Test Your Eyes

Place about ten small objects, such as a key or a penny, on a tray or in a shallow cake pan. Have a friend look at the objects while you count to fifty. Then ask your friend to close his or her eyes. Take away one object. Then have your friend look at the objects again and try to figure out what is missing. Continue with the game until only a few objects are left.

"Eye"-witness Report

Make a chart that shows the eye color of everyone in your family. Fold a piece of paper in half, the long way, and then print the names on one side and draw a picture that shows that person's eye color on the other half. Does everyone in your family have the same color eyes? How many have brown eyes? How many have blue or green or some other color eyes?

Animal Eyes

Visit a pet store to get a close-up look at hermit crabs, fish, lizards, and cats or kittens. Can you see the stalks that support the hermit crab's eyes, or the shiny surface of a cat's eye? Do all the lizards have eyes like the gecko in this book? Compare the ways in which the eyes of the different animals are alike and how they are different.

The Eyes Have It!

How are the eyes of all the animals in this book well suited for their habitat, the place where they live? Can you think of any other animals with eyes that help them survive? For example, hawks have the best vision of any animal. As they fly, their keen eyesight helps them locate prey on the ground.

More Books to Read

Animal Senses. Animal Survival (series). Michel Barré (Gareth Stevens)
Cats. Animals Are Not Like Us (series). Graham Meadows (Gareth Stevens)
Discovering Reptiles and Amphibians. Stephen Cautlin (Troll Associates)
Eyes and Ears. Mark J. Rauzon (Lothrop, Lee & Shepard)
Fish. Wonderful World of Animals (series). Beatrice MacLeod (Gareth Stevens)
Flies. The New Creepy Crawly Collection (series). Tamara Green (Gareth Stevens)
Seeing. Exploring Our Senses (series). Henry Pluckrose (Gareth Stevens)

Videos

All About Eyes. (Agency for Instructional Technology)
Eyewitness: Sight. (DK Vision)
How Animals See. (Wood Knapp Video)

Web Sites

www.aqua.org/animals/species/bluecrab.html
www.eyenet.orb/public/anatomy.html

Some web sites stay current longer than others. For further web sites, use your search engines to locate the following topics: *cats, eyes, fish, frogs, geckos, insects, lizards, reptiles, starfish,* and *vision.*

INDEX